HER

A Book for Women

Seeing Your Self-Worth through the Eyes of God, Not Man

Eduardo D'Angel Vallecillo

ISBN 978-1-0980-5780-0 (paperback)
ISBN 978-1-0980-5782-4 (digital)

Christian Faith Publishing, Inc.
832 Park Avenue
Meadville, PA 16335
www.christianfaithpublishing.com

Printed in the United States of America

Introduction

Hello, I hope you're doing just great. This book is for every woman in the world with no exceptions of color, shape, size, race, for every women was created with the same love—God's love. The cover of this book shows you lots of beautiful red roses and one different, a white rose, that can be you. Once you start believing in the purpose of why God created you, you will finally see yourself like God sees you. I hope this book can give you a little bit of guidance, comfort, and a sprinkle of wisdom. You are wonderfully and perfectly made by the hand of God. You are beautiful in His sight. No man could add any value to you because you are worth far more than rubies. May the Lord enlighten your understanding to help you see how unique you were created to be. No matter what you might think of yourself nor the negative things others might have said contrary to God's word. The reality of the matter is that you were created in God's image.

Her

God didn't want to leave men alone, so His greatest creation came to existence. She was created from his rib close to his heart. She is a perfect fit under his arm so she could be hugged and protected. She is strong like an oak tree but fragile like a rose. She is sentimental and emotional but brave enough to take on the challenge of being a single mother. She is royalty, the daughter of the true King. She is more beautiful than all the flowers in the field. She is more precious than any rubies or diamonds. Her crown is fitted, so it won't fall down if she puts her head down. She was made unique with so many beautiful qualities. The way she loves will always be supernatural.

Single Mother

I want to dedicate this page to all single mothers and let you know God loves you so much.

Being a mother has never been easy. Now imagine being a single mother. I know the road is harder than being just a mom because you double the work. Your circumstances, struggles, problems, from work or home may get you upset, angry, and may get you in a bad mood. Just remember that your children are beautiful blessings from the Lord looking up to you, waiting to be loved. I know it's hard trying to raise kids by yourself, allow me to share part of my childhood with you. Growing up in a household where both my parents worked wasn't easy. They were together, but both work. I had everything but not much attention nor love because they were too busy working. I hardly saw them. I know with work and maybe school, there is no time for you to spare. If you can't make it about quantity, make it about quality. Hug your kids and tell them you love them. They grow so fast, so treasure those little moments with them. Remember your kids are not fatherless as long as you show them the love of our father Jesus Christ. Strengthen yourself in the Lord. Remember with God on your side, everything is possible. When you feel down, pray and read your Bible. The Word of God will guide you and give you peace. Pray, for it will relax you. Pray and trust in God for He will lead you. When the time comes and you have that faith up, He will bring that special man into your life, but all you have to do is trust, love, have faith, and be patient. Let God lead you in everything you do because God is love.

Oh, heavenly Father, I am asking You to protect all of these beautiful mothers on their journey. We know being single is just a stage of their life, for nothing is permanent, and we know that when Your time is right, You will give all of these ladies a wonderful man who will help, lead and love them for who they are. Oh, God, keep their kids and babies safe and protected. If a moment of sadness comes, please, Lord, embrace, and love them, for they are your daughters. They are your princesses. God, keep them healthy, keep them focus, and stretch their time so they can love their beautiful blessings called kids. In Your name, we pray, Jesus Christ. Amen.

Her Protection

I can sit here and quote verse after verse, go religious, but I am not going to do that. I will say it how it is.

If you are a true believer of the *Almighty Living God, Jehovah*, know that a man also needs protection not because he's not strong or because he's not wise but because he needs the protection, the blessing, and the prayers of his partner, his rib, his wife.

Morning prayer
Afternoon prayer
Evening prayer
Nighttime prayer

When times get hard and tough, let him know and make him feel loved. Men at times need to know that they have a safe place in their woman. *Like a game of chess, the queen always protects the king.*

Love Triangle

No, it's not what you think. The love triangle is a relationship between God, man, and woman. Both of them have the same purpose in life, and it's about always putting God first and putting Him in everything they do.

Women tend to think that they are supposed to be like man, but in reality, her role is more important. A woman is the contrast that a man needs to be able to shine.

When a man loves a woman, it is because he becomes more like Jesus and knows his role in marriage and not because of the efforts of a wife trying to change him.

The husband and wife should pray for each other. They should respect each other and honor each other. They are one flesh, and this becomes a way different relationship, not just intimate but also spiritually. A couple that prays together will see the hand of God working on the unity of both.

A love triangle
Won't lie
Won't quit
Won't disrespect
Won't insult
Won't hurt
But will always work together to fix everything that is wrong with the relationship.

If God is with them,
Love will be victorious.

Everlasting

What makes an everlasting relationship?

The main word is *love*.

When true love is found, you will have like a soup of *love*.

You have ingredients that are critical for the soup to be a love soup.

1. Respect
2. Communication
3. Honesty
4. Trust
5. Support
6. Teamwork
7. Encouragement
8. Care
9. Playfulness

These are some of the most critical ones I know. I probably left a few good ones out.

All of this will need to be added to the relationship for love to be *victorious* in the relationship.

And for all my males out there, once you start reflecting Christ's love, you will start loving your one woman because you know that she is to be sheltered under your wing, under your care.

You need to make her feel safe, and over all that, she is loved, and she is very important. If you can't do this for her, rather just leave and don't make her feel unwanted, unloved because God sees her every tear.

Should I Say It?

Okay, here it goes.

Many women desire to marry a man who would wash her feet on their wedding day but end up with guys who don't even want to help them tie their shoes or put their boots on.

They want a man who would not only love them but serve them.

But they end up with men who won't even open a door.

They want a man who is a team player but end up with a man who can't even keep a job.

They want a man who can honor them but end up with a man who verbally abuses them.

A woman was meant to be loved, respected, honored, and protected.

Look at the signs.

If he is not doing it now,

He is more likely not going to do it when you are together.

Slowly examine a man.

Teddy Bear Tears

Late night, I could hear her bedroom door open.

Now the enemy is inside her room, but who can help her if she's alone?

I can hear her screaming, asking her uncle to stop.

Who does he think he is stealing her innocence away?

Night after night, hiding the secret because she felt no one would believe her or even care.

I was the witness of her endless nights.

I could see how she was miserable at times. Her sadness turns into depression, now trying to take her life away.

How could I help if I was only the teddy bear with tears in his eyes?

More than 70 percent of child sexual abuse is committed by someone in the family or close to the family. Talk to your kids if you feel something is different with them.

If you have been abused, remember that what happened to you is not your fault, and you are not what has been done to you but what Jesus Christ will do or has done for you. When you are abused, it brings shame and the feeling of being worthless, but you need to know that what matters is what God says you are and not what the enemy tells you that you are.

And I pray,
Father God,
I lift anyone and everyone
Who has been abused as a child,
Father God,

I put in Your hands every child, protect them, cover them with Your blood, maintain them in the palm of Your hand.

I come against depression, anxiety, self-hate.

I come against demonic forces.

I come against evil spirits.

Fire of God rain in every home.

Let the enemy run away as Your name is announced in every home.

Oh God, be the light that shines in every home.

In the name of Jesus Christ, I pray. Amen.

Surround yourself with those who have the same mission as you.
Make changes when it comes to you,
Your emotions,
Your feelings,
Your thoughts.
If your depressed, sad, lonely, or even mad,
Stay away from negative and pessimistic people,
Stay away from depressing music,
Stay away from the negative environments. Surround yourself with people who truly see your worth, people who cheer you up, listen to encouraging music, go to a place that brings you joy, happiness, and positive vibes. Influence yourself with people who lift you up and not bring you down. Welcome positive and cheerful people into your life and reject those who keep you down.

Pray.

Be happy.
Be joyful.
Be blessed.

Words Are Powerful, Why Not Use Them to Lift Someone Up?

Let's use our words to encourage. Let's use our words to lift. Let's use our words to motivate. Let's use our words to make somebody special. Let's stop putting each other down. Let's help each other be better people. Let's change the way we treat each other, the way we see each other, and the way we talk about each other. Make a difference in a friend, family, coworker, or even a stranger. You have the power in you. Use it to lift, motivate, encourage because one day, you will need the same.

All Single Women, Focus On Being a Better You So You Can Attract a Better Next

I know I have a few female friends who are single. Keep calm, respect yourself, love yourself, motivate yourself, and be positive. Don't make your crown smaller just because a man can't handle you as the queen. Glow with inner beauty and not just only outer beauty. Once you change the way you see life for yourself, you will start to see the kind of man you are attracting. Don't worry, sit back, and wait, for the right man will come to you. Ask, pray, believe, have faith.

Respect Every Women

It always makes me feel sad and upset to see a man mistreating a woman either physically, verbally, emotionally, or mentally. Men, if you're mad or angry, walk away because you can do a lot of damage that can have a very bad result for her. Once you say something you don't mean because of anger, you can't take it back. Never call her names. All women are beautiful regardless of color, size, race, or age. Remember you have a mother, a grandmother, a sister, and someday daughters, and if you think they deserve respect, the same goes to the lady in front of you. You can't have an angel without making a heaven for her. You can't have a queen without making her feel like royalty. Respect her because eventually you will end up alone. God bless all ladies in the world. Take your place, respect yourselves, and if he can't treat you right and understand you, move on. You deserve respect and being treated like a queen.

Flowers

Even all flowers are different they come in different sizes, shapes, colors, and even different floral scents. They are all beautiful just like all women. In order to see a flower grow, you need to water and take care of it because if you mistreated it, it dries and dies. You got to shower your woman with love every day, treat her right so she won't dry or die just like a flower. Remember if you don't take care of your little flower, there will be somebody who will like to bring that beautiful flower back to life.

Don't Hold On Because You Think There Will Be No One Else

How sad it is to see someone in pain, suffering for another person. Most of us at one time, have given it all for that person we thought was that special one in our life. We have ended in tears and sadness, sometimes even physically, mentally, and verbally hurt and abused. You need to come to a point in your life in which you need to realize you control, your happiness. You are the special one. They are losing you, and you're not losing them. You gave that person everything without asking for anything in return, and all they do is hurt you, treat you bad, sometimes cheat on you, or even abuse you in any kind of way. Why would you give them that satisfaction to see you sad, depressed 'cause they left? If they leave or you leave them, you got nothing to lose and everything to gain. I know it hurts. I've been there, done that, but being sad and depressed is hurting you. Don't give anyone the key to your happiness. Keep it with you at all time. Love yourself and not only believe but realize that you are priceless. You are worth every single hug and every single kiss in every single moment that someone special out there is dying to give you. Be calm, relax, and breath. Love will come to you 'cause you deserve every single inch of happiness that is coming your way. Remember, love yourself to the fullest and always smile make them wonder why you are happy and not broken down. God bless you and protect you.

How Do You See Yourself?

What goes through your mind when you see yourself in the mirror? Do you say, "I am so fat, ugly, skinny, short, depressed, sad?" How do you think people would see you if you were a prostitute, drug addict, drunk, or even poor? Well, none of that matters to God because He sees you different than how you see yourself and others see you. God sees potential! God sees beauty because He created you in His image. Not even angels were created in His image. Love yourself, and if you're a lost soul or hating yourself because of your looks or your present situation remember, He knows you are a beautiful soul. Just know that if someone comes close to you and starts to tell you about God it's because He sent that person to try to get you to better yourself for the good not bad. He loves you and cares for you. Smile God knows you're beautiful.

Priceless Jewel

How much is a ruby worth?
All depends on the size.
How much is a sapphire worth?
All depends on the size.
How much is a diamond worth?
All depends on the size.
How much is a precious and beautiful jewel of God?
It's priceless.
No man can buy her.
No man can bribe her.
No man can persuade her.
She knows she is priceless.
She knows in God's eyes, she is worth more than any jewel.
Value yourself, for your price was paid in full with His life.
Believe you are a priceless jewel.
"She is far more precious than jewels" (Proverbs 31:10).

Stop Playing God

Not trying to step on any toes.

I see so many women out there trying to play Jesus.

How many times does a man have to show a woman his true colors?

How many times does it take for women to realize that a chameleon can change colors?

How many times do you need to color a man your favorite color?

How many times do you need to feel worthless?

How many times do you need to feel left out?

How many times do you need to feel unwanted?

Stop trying to change a man. Only two things change a man.

A man will change because he wants to change, but big chance he will go back.

Only God will change a man.

The change is when he understands that he will be accountable for every time he hurt a woman.

He will change because he is fearful of God.

Stop playing God.

Take control of your life.

Pray. Meditate.

Let go. Let God. Stop trying to repaint those that have shown you their true colors.

Lonely Rose

I saw it today.
Unwanted, unloved, lonely. She's beautiful but fragile.
She's gorgeous but delicate,
Beautiful to admire,
But dangerous to touch.
She is covered with extra thorns,
Keeping her guard up,
Keeping anyone from cutting her off.
You can tell she's been hurt before.
Look into her petals; some are damaged; some are cut off.
But that doesn't take away from her beauty.
Lonely rose,
Your sweet fragrance,
Your soft petals,
Your beautiful color
Makes you precious.
If anyone wants you,
They really need to
Be patient and get to know
How to handle you.

Just like this beautiful rose,
You need to keep your guard up.
You need to cover yourself with
God's protection.
And whoever wants you, make sure they know how to handle you.

Man on Fire for God

As I listen to my friend and the situation she is going through, I realize that women are more afraid of having a serious relationship. Heartbreak after heartbreak, I see how important it is to have a man on fire for God.

A man on fire for God understands where he needs to stand when it comes to his partner. He understands that he needs to have the wisdom to guide her and lead her. He needs to have a heart on fire for God to love her as much as he can. He needs to be a protector and hold her when she is afraid, sad, stressed, or even angry. A man on fire realizes that his woman needs to feel loved and wanted, that she is a priority for him, not just another option.

He is so on fire for God and knows that everything bad done, will be accounted for on judgment day; he is fearful of God. A man on fire will be a provider and understands the needs of his woman, not only economical but also emotional, sentimental, physical, and, most importantly, spiritual.

He will try to love her as much as God loves her because he knows he is a reflection of the Most High God.

I know many women have the question, "Well, where is he?" Let me tell you He is not just anywhere. He is not hiding, but he's not in the place where the other fools hang around. Stop looking for pretty boys with cute faces and nice bodies because those men are full of pride. Those men are bashful and know that many women are looking. Stop looking for bad boys and stop pretending you don't know they only want one thing.

A man on fire will wait and knows that God's timing is perfect. The most beautiful thing about a man on fire is that he cares for your life in this world as much as he cares for your eternity. A man on fire will pray for you day after day because he knows that he can't be with you twenty-four seven, but he has faith that God is with you when he is not.

A small clue to identify a man on fire (you will find him mostly alone because he loves his time to meditate, pray, and his time alone with God).

Husband and Wife

Meditate about it.

Your mother and father have always loved you because you have always been their son or daughter.

Your brothers and sisters have loved you because you have been the same to them.

Your children love you because you are their mother or father.

But your wife or husband love you because of you, the person that you are, even in the dark, someone unknown who came into your life and accepted the commitment of becoming one. A wife or husband should be a best friend. Someone who lives day by day with you and together experience crazy, funny, and sometimes sad and tough moments together. So before you think of betraying that person for a good time or maybe to get anger out of you, remember that person has loved you for you and not because they are related to you. A total stranger came into your life to make a lifetime commitment and sacrifice. Respect and love each other, not only from me but it's also a commandment from God.

God be with each and every one,
All couples, husbands and wives.
God bless all of the marriages.

A Letter from Him

Writing to you because every time I try talking to you, I always get
your rejection.

I've seen your suffering because you rather love him and not love me.

I've seen your sadness because he's always putting you aside.

I've seen you make the same mistake begging for love, trying to get
his attention.

I've seen you texting him, telling him that you need him, that he's
like oxygen to you.

Let me tell you something. The reason he's not around is because I
removed him from your life, not to hurt you but because you
deserve better.

I am your God, always taking care of you and loving you.

I am here to hear you.

I am here to guide you.

I am here to shelter you.

I am your God, and if you put me in your heart first,

I will take care of the rest.

Remember I love you. I gave my life for you. All I ask is that you give
me your heart.

I know fake love is everywhere.

But God's love is unconditional.

Refuge in His love and He will find the right man to love you accord-
ing to his heart.

You Got Nothing to Lose

You don't need to show all your pain, for He knows how much you
suffer.

You don't need to show how lonely you are; He knows your emptiness.

You don't need to show a fake smile, for He knows the sadness in you.

You don't need to show your eyes, for He knows how much you have
cried.

Yes, He is the God who loves you and watches over you.

Yes, He is the God who will restore you and put back your broken pieces.

Yes, He is the God who knows your heart and gives you what you need.

Come close to God. You have nothing to lose, and if you lose, you
will lose pain, suffering, and sadness.

Embrace God, and He will restore you.

You can come broken, sad, upset, angry, stressed, anxious, or
depressed. He will help you go through your storm.

All you have to do is come to God. *Come close to God, and God will
embrace you.*

She Knows She Is Not Alone

She doesn't beg for love because the one who loves her will love her without asking.

She doesn't force anyone to stay because whoever wants to stay will stay because they enjoy her presence.

She won't chase no one because she knows her worth and value. She understands that she's the daughter of the King.

Instead—

She prays that she has wisdom to distinguish the truth from the fake. She prays that she is guided in God's ways.

She works not on materialistic things, but on knowing her self-worth and on being the light for others.

She has faith that her heavenly Father will be with her in the good and bad times. She has faith that God will shelter her from harm.

Understand one thing: God loves you, and you don't have to force Him to love you. You don't have to chase Him to stay with you and no need to beg for attention and love because He is waiting with arms wide open to love you. Believe that if you stay faithful and obedient, He will open many doors including ones that seem to be impossible to reach.

She doesn't beg, force, nor chase. She prays, works and has faith.

Love

Love is for husbands and wives.

Love is for your friends and neighbors.

Love is for your kids and family.

Love is for everyone around you.

Love has never been an option.

Love has always been a commandment.

God said go love one another.

Seeking first the good in others.

You should love your neighbors as much as you love yourself.

Because love does no wrong to anyone, but helps in everyday struggles and lifts people up.

Loving others shows how much respect and love you have for God.

If you don't love others, you really haven't known God, for God is love.

If someone is walking in God's path who is wealthy and sees another brother struggling to survive and does nothing, how can they say that they know God? God's love is not in them! Jesus gave His life because of His love for us. God loves us all that He lets the sun shine for the unjust and righteous. Let love be something contagious, that if people see you showing love, they want to do the same. Let's be obedient and love each other and start lifting each other up.

Let's stop using the word *love* like it's meaningless. If you love, show it with behavior and actions.

John 17:21–23

A word of advice.
Make a list of people you don't like.
And pray for them on every day basis.
Watch what happens.

Don't Poison Their Mind

Yesterday, as we walked into the store, my children and I listened as a young mother with four small children on the shopping cart screamed and cursed at her kids.

Her language was just out of control it went from stupid to dogs, to idiots and many other words I'd rather not say.

My sixteen-year-old and my eleven-year-old just turned around and looked at me like in disbelief at what she was saying.

I know that life's circumstances, stress, anxiety, and even depression can get a parent angry and paranoid. Sometimes a fight with the boyfriend, husband, friends, or even family can trigger anger and stress. Just like an overheated car trying to release pressure, mothers and fathers blow up at this lil persons who can't defend themselves.

Remember, once the words are out, you can't get them back, and it's easy to poison a child with hateful words. Unfortunately, the person who is supposed to bring comfort and love shows them hate and anger. The kids wonder if Mom or Dad really love them.

I am not here to point fingers, but if you have ever allowed hate, anger, stress, or conflict rule over you,

Stop, think, and take control before it controls you. Distract your mind on something that can calm you down.

Love your children, make them feel safe and protected; they grow too fast.

I don't know this young mom, but one thing for sure, I've been praying for her so much.

Find This Man

Find a man who protects you.

Physically—who keeps you away from harm and danger.
Mentally—who keeps you away from a toxic environment and doesn't abuse you verbally.
Emotionally—who speaks to you with a voice that comforts you and makes you feel welcome to talk to him.
Sexually—who he respects, has self-control, and doesn't make you feel like an item they just use.
Spiritually—he will lead you to God because he knows the importance of a relationship with God. He will pray with you and for you because he knows that you need that communication with the living God who brings protection to a couple.

Find a man who provides. We live in a society in which females are independent and willing to work and provide for themselves. If this man can show you he's secure and can provide for you as a man, he's showing you that he can be responsible, and is not only a boy trying to play games.

Find a man who makes you a priority. This man will handle his business and try to finish work, hobbies, or duties just to give you the time you deserve.

This man is allowed to have some fun with friends, watch sports, and have some time for himself, but he will know when to put everything aside to be with his woman.

Find a man who takes initiative. This man will not just sit around; he will take the lead and try to find solutions to problems.

He will take the lead and find ways to keep the relationship going in the right direction, not because woman can't do it but because he will go beyond to see his woman smile.

This man will create a safe environment for you. He will protect you, prioritize you, lead you, and respect you.

Make sure you open your eyes
Because God will lead this man to you.

Your job will be to separate the good from the bad. Read the Word of God, pray, and you will eventually learn and understand what to look for in a man.

Ladies, I can assure you that there are still men like that. I personally know a few loyal, faithful, and godly men.

Like I said, pray, meditate, and read the Bible.

God will show you how to know which one he is.

Stop falling in love with the same kind of men.

No words Needed.

No words needed when actions speak louder than words.

Unfortunately, we live in a society that is more afraid of losing their phones than losing their wallets or purses.

People live with their phones stuck to their hands.

So if he doesn't text, it's simple. You're not a priority.

Takes ten seconds to open the phone, write good morning, how are you, good night, etc.

Stop pretending that he cares.

Stop believing he couldn't.

Stop closing your eyes to reality.

You can't make a man

Love you,

Care for you,

Give you attention,

Give you his time,

So stop asking! All of that needs to be given at his free will.

Pray and ask God

To lead you,

To guide you,

To give you wisdom,

To give you understanding,

To give you strength

And the ability to pick right from wrong.

The love that you will always have is found in Christ.

All you need is to say, "Father, hold me and embrace me."

No man is worth your tears. And if you cry, remember who is there to catch your tears (God).

Communication is the Key.

If we don't say what we feel, no one will ever hear us.

Some problems in life and marriage can be solve with simple communication.

Mature communication between husband and wife, girlfriend and boyfriend, even friends starts with focusing on the problem, not the person. It's not about pointing fingers but rather getting together to see what's missing, how can we agree. What could we do to solve the problem? The key word here is *we* together as a team. Issues come and go, but there is nothing that two people willing to fight can't do to keep the relationship alive. Tell your partner your likes, your dis-likes, what makes you happy, what makes you sad, what makes you angry. Have conversations, ask each other questions that will help you get to know each other to the fullest. I know of couples who have been together for a long time and still don't even know 50 percent about their partner, this is sad but true.

Make your better half your best friend.

Think Before You Get Hurt

Like they say, wipe those tears and move on. There's plenty of fish in the sea. Yes, it's true that there is also trash in the sea, but you can always distinguish the trash and move it to the side.

The problem is when you want the fish that you find beautiful in your eyes but it's a fish that is trash. Literally speaking, some of the most beautiful fish in the sea are toxic, poisonous, or very aggressive.

Now back to figuratively speaking, you need to really get to know some of these fish and not catch one right away, or you could end up hurt. Make the right choice even if you have to wait.

Pray to God for wisdom, patience, and discernment to guide you through this ocean of where only the strong and wise survive.

God bless you and be with you always. *There's plenty of fish in the sea, but there's also lots of trash.*

Strong Mind

How do we get better at doing things?

Training always makes you better at what you want to accomplish.

Circumstances and life events are responsible for our emotions whether it's good or bad. It all depends on how we take them in.

You lost your job.

You lost your house.

You got divorced.

And the list goes on and on.

It has always been a difficult life.

I can sit here and go on and on to try to motivate and help you, but it's not on me. It's on you and what you want your mind to believe.

Now from my part, let me tell you how to make a strong mind.

You sit down alone, meditate, then pray, ask God for guidance, then you read the Bible, and write what you learn. There is so much knowledge, so much wisdom in God's Word.

You will never ever start thinking better or get a stronger mind if you keep the same thoughts and same mentality.

Believe me, it's hard, but it's worth it. Putting God on your mind will help you through life in so many ways.

He is the only one who can help you gain control of your emotions and your life.

Broken Wings

A little honeybee with broken wings would go out every day to collect honey and pollen.

She was the last one to get back almost empty due to her shaking while flying.

She felt worthless. She felt disappointed because she couldn't be like the rest.

The queen called her.

"Dear, what's wrong? Why are you upset?"

She replied,

"I can't seem to do anything right. I am the last one to get here, and the one that brings less."

The queen said,

"Come, let's fly, show me the path you take home."

Admired by the beauty of the path, the queen was surprised.

The queen said, "Look, dear, at how beautiful this path is, full of colorful flowers. This is all possible due to your broken wings, if you hadn't drop all of this pollen on your way home, there wouldn't be any flowers. In the near future, you will see others collecting pollen and honey. Thanks to you. Thanks to your broken wings."

Never feel worthless just like that little bee.

God will always use you in great ways regardless of your imperfections and defects.

God loves you no matter what.

All you have to do is ask God to guide you and lead you.

Make a difference in others. Humble your heart.

Be a Lion

I see so many posts of woman trashing each other, especially calling each other female dogs.

You need to remain wise. It's better to be like a lion and ignore the barks of a dog.

Always put your trust in God and let Him handle those who do you wrong. Keep your face forward, smile, and ignore because you know who has your back.

When a dog barks and you respond, guess what? You bark back. Remember let the dog be a dog. You keep on being a lion and put your trust in God.

The Influence of a Strong Woman in a Man

One night, Obama and his wife, Michelle, decided to go for a casual dinner at a restaurant that wasn't too luxurious. When they were seated, the owner of the restaurant asked if he could please speak to Michelle. Michelle had a conversation with the owner. Following this conversation, President Obama asked Michelle, "Why was he so interested in talking to you?" She mentioned that in her teenage years, he had been madly in love with her. Obama then said, "So if you had married him, you would now be the owner of this lovely restaurant," to which Michelle responded, "No, if I had married him, he would now be the president."

If you have a man, be a strong support for him, encourage him, push him, motivate him, and support him with his goals and dreams. At the end, it's not only about what he accomplishes but what the both of you were able to do as a team. A man is as strong as his support. Imagine if I had a Michelle, I would've finished my two books and started on my clothing company. Eventually I'll get there little by little.

God bless every couple trying to reach their goals together.

God, lead the way.

God, be the solid rock and the foundation for those dreams to become a reality.

Peace

Sometimes it's beautiful outside, and we enjoy dancing in the rain.

What happens when we get a full storm with nowhere to run or hide?
Many will cry, many will panic, many will lose faith, and some just give up.

Life brings unexpected tragedies, unexpected problems.

Life has ups and downs.

Sometimes people we love go against us; people we care for hurt us.

What do we need to do to find that peace?

Well, first step is pray to God for strength and understanding then pray some more for guidance and wisdom.

Remain, firm on the rock (God).

Take a deep breath and believe that God will take you out of the storm. God will give you wisdom, strength, and guidance.

Being at peace doesn't mean that everything is perfect and calm. Being at peace means that you can breathe calmly, believing everything will be okay because God is holding your hand.

Without You

You love me without deserving it.
You hug me and embrace me even though I'm no one special.
You pick me up and save me from dark places.
Now
I am nobody without You.
Without You, I am just another hopeless sinner.
Without You, I am lost in the world.
I don't want to live life without out You.

Thank You, Father, for taking care of me in every step I take.

Your Happiness

I wish I could underline the title so I could make many people understand and see that your happiness is yours, and you shouldn't let anyone steal it from you. I know at times, others are not very nice and treat you bad. Remember that if someone is mean, disrespectful, arrogant, selfish, or negative, there is something wrong with them not you. Don't let that steal your happiness nor peace. Keep that smile up and guard *your happiness*.

God sends the blessings, and it's our duty to appreciate them and fuel our happiness with them.

Look at what you have and not what you don't have.

Remember there is always someone out there praying for a few things you have that we as humans take for granted.

I ask God to give me happiness. God said, "No, I am giving you blessings. Happiness is up to you."

Real Queens Fix Each Other's Crowns

What situation has been your biggest battle? That at one point had power over your life, and now you can say, "Thank God because I am not there anymore."
You were an
Alcoholic woman,
Drug-addict woman,
Unhappy woman,
Or
A woman sexually, physically, or mentally abused.
You're a
Widow woman,
Single woman,
Or married woman
Doesn't matter.
Who are you? Who were you?
What you do from now on is what matters. God will transform your moments of pain, your tragic memories into victories for other women.
Your testimony, your victories can be used to help women guide themselves to make their situation much easier.
Open a group maybe, a ministry in your church.
Glorify God together.
The victory will be yours with God at your side.
Reach and stretch one hand to fallen women and one shoulder to sad women.
You are all God's queens.
Fix each other's crowns.

You Reply to His Message When You Said You Were Not Going to Talk to Him No More?

Even though it seems funny, it's very sad.
Why? Because many women can't understand the fact that most men won't change; they will continue doing what they like doing.
Let's hit it. Quit it. I don't have anything to hit. Let's call her again. Let me tell her she looks fine, and that I miss her. I hit it. She got boring. Bye. If she looks good again, I may hit it again.
Come on, ladies, clear your mind, meditate, pray, and respect yourselves.
God gave you great value.
God knows how much you're worth don't settle for men's mind games.

They say fool me once shame on you,
Fool me twice shame on me
The shame will always be on the person enjoying the game.
But you as a woman need to put a stop to the childish games, you're the one who will hurt the most at the end.

Put your focus on God's love, and you will understand how much you are loved and how much you are worth.

Hope

It's hard having dreams when all hope is gone.
Once your hope is gone, life tends to be worthless.

Hope for a cancer patient is another day to live.
Hope for a blind person is to have surgery, blink, and see light.
Hope for a soldier's mother is to see her son coming back from war.
We go to sleep with hopes of a new beginning, a new day.

Hope goes hand in hand with faith.
Faith is the trust you put in God, and feed with your hopes.

God bless you always.
Let my Lord give you strength and guidance.

Faith

For all my trust is in You, Lord.
Always pray for a new beginning.
In good and bad, You're here with me.
Take my insecurities and doubts.
Honor to Your name, God, I will.

She Asked

Baby, what am I worth?

He replied,
To any other man, not much, maybe they can put a money value on
 you.

To me, my love, you are priceless. I couldn't repay what you've done
 for me.

To God, well, to Him, you are worth His life.
So imagine that.
Your worth is infinite like His love.
She smiled like never before.

Lord, Forgive Me, but It's Time to Go Back to the Old Me

How sad is it to give up and to let go of God's hand because you were not strong enough to deal with the people or circumstances that are tormenting you at that given time. To run away from the storm because you couldn't handle getting slammed with the wind and water.

Don't give people or circumstances the power over your emotions, especially the power to control your love for God.

At that moment, you may feel that you're going to break, but God will pick you up and shelter you when He knows you're ready.

In order for a sword to be super strong, it needs to have gone through the fire a couple of times.

Whatever you do, never go back to the place where God picked you up from. Never look back, and if you fall, get up and keep on moving.

God gives us a new day every day, no reason to go back to the old you. If that hasn't worked your whole life, what makes you think it will work now? God will change things for you on His time, just make sure you are ready.

God bless you.
Stay strong.
Stay positive.
And don't give your power to anyone but God.

Ladies, Wait for a Man Who...

Works—Well, he needs to provide for his queen even though he knows that she can provide for herself. It's something he would love to do with pleasure.

Lives the Bible—Living in God's way will show him to respect her and follow rules that will make his relationship with her a successful one.

Prays—He will pray for her because he knows that God will protect her and keep her safe when he's not around. He will pray for her success, her health, and her soul.

Worships—Because he's thankful that God gave him his other half and made them one. He glorifies God because He's an amazing God.

Becoming Mr. Right

A man once asked his father, "Father, how will I ever find the right woman?" His father replied, "Forget finding the right woman, focus on being the right man." This happened to me with my friend.

He was telling me, "Look, Eddie, I am tired of being alone, tired of not having someone around. I want a woman with a good heart who likes to cook, who knows everything about me, and we can laugh at crazy things. I want her to have a great body, beautiful face, a peaceful attitude, and that she is smart and supports me on what I do."

My reply was, "Everything sounds great, sounds like your dream woman. Now let me ask a question, are you a man that your dream girl will like in her life? Are you ready to please her in every way? Are you ready to leave all the bad habits? Are you ready to change your temper? Are you ready to stop playing games? Are you ready to be mature and become the man she needs?"

Silence.

Before you go into a serious relationship, ask questions, get to know each other, find out if he is the man you need.

And yes, it works both ways.

Don't Settle For A Church Boy

There's a huge difference between a guy who goes to church with you once a week; from a man who encourages your walk with Christ daily.

A man can impress a woman by telling her, "It's Sunday. Let's go to church, babe." Just remember, Jesus kicked out a demon from church because he felt comfortable.

A real godly man will lead, motivate, and encourage you to have a better relationship with God. He will pray with you, and he will pray for you. He will never put himself first, but he will put God first. He will grab your hand and together follow and serve God.

We Evolve

As time passes by, we evolve into coldhearted creatures.

We forget about love.

We forget about care.

We forget to be humble.

We walk by the homeless veterans who, one day, served us, but we are not humbled enough to serve them since they can't serve us anymore.

We decide to lock our parents up in nursing homes because we don't want them to be another cross to carry, but they never locked us up when we were children.

We rather record a little girl jumping off a building than to reach out, help her, and let her know there is always hope.

We make memes of pictures with disabled people, then we laugh and share like it's something funny.

We can't find love because we don't know what it looks like anymore.

We spend hours on our phones that we forgot how to interact and teach our children respect and love. We give them a tablet or a phone just so that they could give us time and space to be on our phones.

We'd rather share videos of people killing each other.

We'd rather share sexual post.

We enjoy and like chaos and gossip.

We stay away from positive post.

And we wondered why the world is what it is.

We evolve for the worst.

Our hearts are cold and solid like rocks.

Earnestly I pray,
Oh heavenly Father,
Forgive us, for we don't know what we are doing.
Forgive us for not being the light that guides each other.
Forgive us because we spread hate rather than spreading love.
O Father, I know you forgive us, I ask that you give us guidance and
    wisdom to do what's right.
O Father, empty every single drop of negativity and hate and fill us
    up with your love so we can go and spread it to the world.
In the Name of Jesus Christ I pray
Amen and Amen.

Venting

I see so many people venting on Facebook and social media.

It would be great if we could read minds. Then would we know that most of these people love to feed from people's problems and bad circumstances. The bigger the problem, the better the gossiping.

They say, "I am so sorry you are going through this," but in their minds, they're like, "She deserves this and more for being how she is."

Only a true friend which is hard to find, will always be there to support you and give you advice on how deal with your problems and circumstances.

So many people may care a little, but they're not willing to invest time and effort in problems or bad circumstances that don't belong to them. So it's like they don't care.

The only thing you do by venting on Facebook and social media is giving people a show that they love to watch. People have become so cold and heartless that they'd rather watch you die and get a like than to stretch out their hands and get you out. To them, watching you die is more entertaining.

Word of advice, post things that are positive and post your happiness even if you're not that way. You don't need to feed those people who enjoy and rejoice in others pain and sorrows.

If you need to vent, please bend your knees and pray. He's the one who really cares. "Never tell your problems to anyone. Twenty percent don't care; the other 80 percent are glad you have them."

Let them judge you and misunderstand you. Their opinions aren't your problem. Never doubt your worth. Just keep on shinning.

Be the light that shines.

Regardless of what people think or say about you, don't give them the power to turn off the light inside of you.

People could continue poisoning each other, but you continue to spread love. At the end of the day the love that comes out of your heart is what matters to God. If you want to mimic them and spread hate, well, you pay them back the same way and become like them.

Don't let others cover your love with hate.

Stand firm, stand strong.

Bless all of those who do you wrong.

Let God judge them.

God will bless and guard your beautiful heart.

You are way better than anger, hate, and negativity.

You are the light, the love, and the positive attitude that can make another person's day go better.

Lost

I was in a very beautiful place,
A place where I could breath and feel at peace.
I was afraid to close my eyes, scared to wake up, and think it might
   be a dream.
I was surrounded by beautiful sparkling lights, pretty just like stars.
It was very calm and peaceful, a place where there was no rush and no
   time.
The more I would explore, the more I would fall in love with this place.
The wind sounded like beautiful melodies.
The rain felt like bursting bubbles.
The ground was softer than any expensive carpet.
This place was beautiful, peaceful, amazing, and breathtaking.
I was stress free with a feeling of being weightless.
Then I realized
I wasn't sleeping.
I wasn't dreaming.
I wasn't dead.
I came to realize that I was lost in the beauty of your mesmerizing
   eyes.

Be Selective

Let me start with two stories as examples.

My friend drives a motorcycle. I asked him a while back if he was a safe driver. He said yes. The next day, he passed me on the freeway superfast. When I saw him, I confronted him, and told him to be careful when driving, not because he doesn't know how to drive but because others are careless drivers. His other friends told him that it was cool to drive fast and cut cars off. They would do the same!

One friend told the other, "Let's go out drinking." The other replied, "No, let's stay home and watch movies with all our kids." She told her, "No, let me ask my other friend." The other friend replied, "Let's go. If we end up in jail, we end up together that's why we are friends."

The first story could end up in a tragedy. Who would pay the price? The family. His body could end up at the hospital or cemetery thanks to his so-called friends, believing that it was the cool thing to do!

The second story has the same outcome or maybe even worse. The person could end up taking a life or spending time in jail.

See, you need to be selective on who you listen too.

Your friend is not the one who can be with you in jail. It's the one who tells you not to do the things that can get you in trouble. Your friend is not the one who agrees with everything you say. It's the one who confronts you concerning your mistakes. Your fake friend will always stab you in the back. Your true friend will stab you in the front with things you hate to hear but are true.

Just like when you're selective with clothes, shoes, and what you drive, be more selective with the people you trust, open your door to, and the ones you call friends. All material stuff you're selective with can always be replaced, but a true friend or a true loved one can't be replaced.

God bless and protect you. Do what feels right, not what you know will get you into trouble.

Word of advice, let God separate you from what keeps you from loving him and others. I'll guarantee you that lots of those no good friends little by little will begin to stay away.

You're Perfectly Made

You shouldn't compare yourselves to anything nor anyone in this world because you're the daughter of a celestial Father. Don't let society and media show you how to be a perfect woman and get you sad and upset because you don't meet their expectations. Be happy and love who you are, and if there is something you don't like, wake up every morning and try to be a better woman than you were the day before. There is no perfect woman; everyone has flaws and defects, but even like that, you are loved unconditionally. Be you and love yourself and remember that your beauty and shine comes from the heart. There is no stronger woman than the one who walks with God.

He Asks and Prays to God

Father, lead me to the perfect wife, but God replies, "Son, don't worry about that, just prepare to be perfect for her. When you are ready, I will walk you through the door that will lead you to her."

Now he knows that he needs to love her not with his mind because many things can make him lose it, not with his heart because it will eventually stop, but with his soul and spirit because it's what stays alive.

Live a relationship where God is first, and you better believe that God will protect your marriage.

Husband, love your wife.

Wife, respect your husband.

O Father, bless everyone who is looking for a soulmate. Prepare them for that special day.

Silent Tears

Once again, I sit alone, while the silent tears rolls down my cheek.

Many numb the pain with alcohol and self-mutilation just like I did once upon a time. Others tend to use drugs to quiet that screaming lament inside, but my favorite was cutting myself to feel physical pain instead of the emotional pain.

I look around at this present moment, desperately needing a hug that no one is willing to give.

I lie in bed. Someone is next to me but can't see my pain, so my pillow catches my silent tears.

Drowning myself in my own pain with no one to understand. Many love to see me in pain, and others don't care.

But is not until I met You and decided to have a personal relationship with You, Lord, that I understood that You love me so much and would wipe away every silent tear.

Thank You, Father, for giving me strength and peace in my heart and for catching every silent tear.

Father, I ask that You have an encounter with every single person who is going through a trial and can't find the solution. Let them experience Your fulfilling love.

Bless them.

Protect them.

Guide them.

Keep them strong.

Under Your Makeup

Your looking amazing. Everything seems in place, just look at that beautiful face.

Every man who walks by you can't help to look and mesmerize over your beautiful eyes.

Only you know how many tears you are hiding behind that makeup.

Maybe the scars of a broken heart.

Under your makeup hides your true life story. Sleepless nights full of pain.

Under your makeup, the deepest secrets hide away that sometimes it doesn't feel like it's enough. The secret of a violent relationship or maybe, the betrayal of the one you loved or maybe the secret of being abused.

Your lipstick gives your smile a gorgeous shine, but it's not a truthful smile.

Your eyeliner makes those pretty eyes stand out and look so deep.

Only if men would realize what's under your makeup, they would realize that love and protection is what you need.

Now it's time for you to run to the arms of the one who loves you unconditionally. He loves you for who you are. Let go and cry in the arms of your comforter, your creator, the lover of your soul which is Jesus Christ. The time will come when He will send you that amazing God-fearing man who will help fix what's behind all that makeup and give you a new beginning. He will get on his knees before the Lord with prayer and supplication concerning healing over your broken heart and soul.

Trust in God with all your heart.

Something Is Missing

Life has changed so much; the most valuable gift from God is missing in us. We are missing love.

We are missing love.

We are missing hugs.

We are missing attention.

We are missing kisses.

The person who just lost a loved one, lost the opportunity to show them how much they love them. Now it's too late to be crying at their grave site.

Run, make time for the ones you love, show them how much they mean to you.

A parent too busy with work, the gym, the socializing, drinking, just lost a child due to suicide, it's too late now for regrets. If they only knew the difference they would've made with a simple hug, a kiss, and time to talk to their loved ones about their lives.

An alcoholic drinking his life away, crying over the fact that he feels lonely without her, she's gone now! All he needed was to stay strong and show her love, affection, and respect.

And many other examples I could give where love could've made the difference.

To the wife,

Hugs, kisses, and love.

To the kids,

Attention, hugs, and love.

To the parents,

Hugs, respect, and love.

To each other,
Helping hand, respect, and love.

If we could just wake our heart up and let all that love radiate through us, we can make so many changes.

A woman should never be struggling financially, spiritually, insecurely, or emotionally with a grown man lying next to her.
Amen.

A man's duty is to
Make her feel safe,
Make her feel secure,
Make her feel beautiful,
Make her feel protected,
Make her feel special,
Make her feel important,
Hug her when she is sad,
Kiss her when she is upset,
Hold her when she is scare,
Compliment her when she is feels ugly,
And at times, be quiet and listen to her. She needs your attention and friendship.

O Father, guide all men who are lost. Give them wisdom and understanding to realize that it's their duty to be the ones to protect, provide, and love their woman.

Pray for each other, men and women.

I Am a Bad Chick

She said, "I am a bad chick who likes bad boys."

That is probably why you stay in bad relationships.

If he turns around to check out your body, just remember he will turn around when another passes by showing more.

Don't look for love or attention in the wrong places because you will end up upset and broken.

Don't forget who you are,

The daughter of a true King.

God loves His daughters.

A Prayer for Her

Heavenly Father, You are worthy to be praised and glorified; I cover her with the precious blood of Jesus Christ. I pray that you bless her with divine health and keep her safe as she lives out each day. I pray for protection over her mind as she reads things on the internet and encounters false teachings. Holy Spirit, protect her mind and keep her wise in the correct direction toward truth. O Lord, I pray the full armor and shield of protection over her. I pray that she is blessed with good health and a body that functions to its fullest potential. I believe and know that even when I am not around, she is protected by Your presence. Lord, I pray that You give her wisdom, focus, and tranquility as she goes day by day. Let her be light so she can guide others. O Father, grant her a pure heart that she stays humble and kind. Lord, protect her from all spiritual attacks, protect her against the efforts of the evil one and his affiliates. I pray that You protect her mind, heart, body, and soul as she walks in this life. In the name of Jesus Christ, I pray.

Amen and Amen.

Husband Benefits

If you want to be a wife, stop giving men husband benefits. Respect yourself.

He wants all your attention with his time limit.
He won't commit because you're letting him get away with it.
He calls you babe so he won't call you another name.
He won't put a ring on your finger because he gets what he wants for free.
He won't pay rent because just like barhopping; he house-hops.
If he wanted to commit, he would, but his life is much easier disrespecting you.
Learn to respect yourself and give yourself that special place. You're not only a woman; you're the offspring of a King, one day to become a queen.

Let God bless you and protect your heart.

A Queen without a King

She cries herself to sleep, thinking and wondering when her time will come, the moment when her king will come to rescue her from that loneliness and emptiness inside her heart.

She would cry every time she saw pictures of her female friends and female family members happy with their husbands.

She would complain to God why not her, why couldn't she have a relationship like that. She would spend nights just wondering and days just daydreaming.

What she didn't know was that 50 percent to 70 percent of couples are not satisfied with their relationship. She didn't know that simple arguments could open doors to infidelity and disrespect. She didn't know everything changes after a picture in most relationships.

God knew that her heart was kind and precious so her being alone wasn't because he wanted her alone. All along it's been because He has been working on putting that man in her life who will be worth all that beauty her heart carries.

Be patient God hears your prayer and catches your tears. Don't try to look for love the same way you always do because you will only be walking in circles.

My Strong Beautiful Pillar

You are my wife, but most importantly, you are my strong beautiful pillar.

You support me when I feel weak. You support me when I feel upset.

I know at times I put so much stress on you to the point of breaking.

You are my strong beautiful pillar that allows me to stand firm and hopeful.

Without your supporting strength, I would be weak and broken.

Not only do you support me, but you make life easier.

Forgive me if at any point in life, I stressed you and put extra weight.

You are my strong beautiful pillar, and together, we make up this home.

Not only are you a strong pillar, but you're beautiful as well.

So all I have to say is thank you for the support and strength you provide.

Another beautiful poem. Thank You, God, for everything.

Dedication goes out to all wives in the world who give that support to their husbands, that no matter the situation, their behind him 100 percent. Keep up the faith.

To all husbands, please thank your wife 'cause little do you know, they're stronger than us in so many ways. Thank God He created them especially for us.

I Know You Are Tired

He looked at her eyes and penetrated all the way to her soul.
He held her and embraced her.
He comforted her.
He wiped her tears.
He healed her pain.
He put her broken pieces back together.
Confused, she said, "Who are you?"
"I am the son of a king who was sent to you with the purpose of lifting you up and giving you strength.
Kneel with me, let's call upon His name, and you will be tired no more."

God loves you without measure, without boundaries.
You only need to give everything to God and let Him carry your load.

Perfect Imperfections

He knew from day one, it was her by the sparkle in her eyes and the connection they had.

Without a search connected by faith,

Falling in love like two young kids in elementary school, and even though it was no game, the love was pure.

She was always shy, but he had a way to make her smile.

Mistreated in her past, he seemed to always make her feel safe regardless of the bad memories from the past.

She would say, "Look at my stretchmarks."

He would reply, "Don't worry. Its' a sign that you're a great mother," then slowly he would kiss them.

She would say, "But look at me. I look ugly without makeup."

He would reply, "Don't worry. Your natural beauty matches your beautiful heart."

She would say, "Look at my hands, full of scars."

He would reply, "You're an amazing woman. The scars are just a reminder of what you've been through and how strong you are."

Hugging her, he would say, "I love every single imperfection in you because it's what makes everything perfect for me."

He became her shoulder, her peace, her safety. She was loved because he love God first, so he knew that was his destiny—to make God's lil queen happy.

Tell Me What Broke You

Tell me, was it a man who mistreated you?
Did he abuse you
Mentally,
Verbally,
Physically?
Tell me, was it an addiction to a substance abuse,
Alcohol,
Drugs,
Pills?
What's breaking you?
Anger,
Pain,
Stress,
Sadness?
Meditate and pray.
Stay strong.
Stay focused.
Do what is right in your heart.
I know many of the times, you go back to what broke you just because
it is easier and simpler.
Lift your arms surrender to God. Let Him
Embrace you,
Hold you,
Heal you,
Love you,
Bless you.
Let go. Let God.

I believe you God

I know you still worry.
I know you still stress.
I know you still cry
Or maybe you're mad or sad.
Life hurts.
Life tends to have its painful moments, and life has ups and downs.

His promise was not for a life in this world to be painless, without worries, or sadness free, but He did promise He would be with you always, good or bad.
He would be your solid rock, and if you have become His child, He will turn anything bad in your life into something you can use for your advantage.

Stop saying
I believe in God.
Remember even the demons believe in God.

Stand with your head looking up and say,
"I believe you, God."

You will see the difference it makes in your life.

God always provides at the right time.
All you need to do is believe God.

If She

If she cries, hold her.
If she's scared, hug her.
If she's mad, calm her down.
If she misses you, call her.
If she doubts, make her believe.
If she's sad, make her laugh.
If she's sick, take care of her.
If she's anxious, hug her.
If she worries, pray with her.
But most of all, never stop loving her.
Surprise her at all times.

The Sun and the Moon

As he meditates and prays for her in the middle of the night, he feels a deep pain and disappointment because he's not around to protect her and keep her safe. He closes his eyes, and tears roll down his face, but he realizes something so beautiful and tells God, "Father, as You know, I can't be there to protect her and keep her safe at all times. O Father, You let the sun give the moon her shine even when they are apart. You let the moon shine with his light even on the darkest nights. O Lord, protect her and giver her Your love so she can shine so bright even in those darkest moments with the power of Your unconditional love."

With a smile on his face, he says amen.

He knows the power of his loving Father.

The Girl and the Apple Tree

Every day, the beautiful girl would stop by the apple tree. She would always grab the ones on the ground. She would wipe them and try to eat them, but it would always be the same, either rotten or putrid. One day, the girl tried to climb the tree. To her surprise, the snake on the tree slid down. "Where are you going, beautiful girl?" She replied, "I am tired of rotten apples. I want to see what's up there." The snake replied, "Get down. You can get hurt, plus these apples are not ready. There super sour and hard. The good ones are on the ground. You just need to try and try and never come up here again. You could be more disappointed than you already are." The beautiful girl climbed down. "You're right. I'll keep on trying. I have nothing to lose."

The next day, the beautiful girl was looking for those good apples when the gardener asked, "Hi, beautiful girl, what are you doing?" She said, "Looking for good apples." He said, "Oh no, sweetheart, all the ones on the floor are bad already. Some even have worms. If you're looking for the good ones, always come to me. I'll get you sweet and juicy ones that I get from up top."

With a look of surprise, she said, "But, sir, the snake said that I could get good one from the ground." The gardener replied, "Oh, sweetheart, that lying snake again. That snake loves to make my apples go bad, but if I see it, I will cut its head off. Come, beautiful girl, let me show you the good apples I got for you." She said, "Oh, sir, these are delicious. I should've waited for you to show me. Give me some of those delicious apples."

How many times have we made the mistake of making a bad choice and keep on doing it time after time? Be patient, ask God for guidance. He always knows what's good for you. The snake will always try to trick you into believing that you will find better in the same place. If after you've tried and tried and it remains the same, it's time to leave it in God's hands even though it may feel like a long time before He brings the right person to you. Everything will be worth the wait 'cause it's perfect when you wait on God's timing.

Dirty Diamond

Rolling on the ground, just another worthless dirty little rock.
People will pass by it, step on it, sometimes even kick the little rock
without knowing its worth.
Men will pick you up and throw you away like a little rock.
To the world, just another worthless dirty little rock without a value.
Then—
He found you, picked you up, cleaned you, and washed you up.
He knew your worth. He knew that you would sparkle and shine.
He knew that it would only take His love and His attention.
He picked you up from all that dirt because He saw the beauty within
      you.
Now you glow with beautiful shine, and men are trying to buy you,
      but He made you priceless because you're perfect to Him now.

God will lift you and make you priceless when everyone else is trying
      to judge you because of where you've been and what you've done.

Shine in His name.
Shine to light others up.

Life Is Like a Boxing Match

Life never tends to be an easy fight, just like a boxing match. In one corner, you're against life's problems and the circumstances it brings. Your problems will always try to knock you down over and over with no consideration.

Train so you can get better at defeating life's problems.

Study the problem and circumstances so it won't get you off guard to hit you and knock you down.

Gain condition so you can last longer standing up and fighting.

The more fights against life, the more experience you get from it.

It's not about how many times those problems can throw you down but how many times and how fast you're willing to get up without giving up. Always have a positive mentality of moving forward.

Discipline yourself.

Train hard and believe in yourself.

You are in pain.

You are suffering.

Get up and win.

If your problem is a giant, remember David, for he did not see the size of Goliath. He saw the size of his God who gave him the courage to move forward, believing in himself. He knew that if God is for us, who can be against us?

God bless you, my champs.

Let's knock some problems down.

You line them up, I knock them down.

Something to think about.

God Protects Even When We Complain

True story. Every day, I get out at 4:30 p.m. from work and run out the door. Today, there was a little bit more work than usual. I could've still left. I decided not to, even my friend commented that it was going to rain. I ended up leaving work at 5:15 p.m. and took my usual route home. As I got closer to the loop I took to get on the freeway it was closed off. As I got closer, I saw a trailer flipped and crushed. What happened? I don't know. I started thinking and talking to God. "Was it You, Father, that somehow managed to keep me at work safe and protected me from an accident happening to me?"

Sometimes we complain about things that happened to us in life, for example, being late to work 'cause you woke up late. Maybe God allowed you to oversleep to protect you. Maybe you passed your exit without realizing it was to prevent you from an accident. God's power is amazing, and it's always fighting for us, but sometimes we'd rather see the negative side of things instead of the positive side. Remember if God has a purpose for you, He won't rest till He makes you understand what that reason is.

Live each day with joy, and remember if you're still awake tomorrow, thank God for it and try your best to find that purpose in your life.

First Impressions

It will be amazing to see everyone's flaws at the beginning, but it's so hard to tell who is who in a world full of people wearing masks. A beautiful story of the beauty and the beast where he shows he's a beast with a beautiful heart, not a handsome man with a heart of a beast, someone who treats you bad and disrespects you. What if we show our bad side first, would those people in our life stay or leave?

Stop falling in love with first impressions. People change, people take off their mask in the worst situations. Take time to know someone. It may take time and patience, but it will be worth it. Why? Because not only would you avoid heartbreak, you will not waste time with the wrong person. Ask a million questions. Try to find everything and anything about that person before you jump into a commitment.

Time plus patience plus communication equals good relationship.

Remember, when life gets hard, take a knee and pray.

Change

I often see mothers screaming and mistreating their kids because they misbehave bad.

I often see people drinking or consuming drugs to forget about the past.

I often see women hurting because they end up with the same kind of men over and over.

I often see people trying to fill up that empty hole within them with self-pleasure that at the end of the day, they always end up feeling lonely.

What makes these people think that their lives will change if they continue applying the same strategy to fight their problems? People need to change their thoughts so that they could be able to change their lives.

Try to surround yourself with positive thoughts and positive influences that will have a good impact on your life.

The Man of God and the Snake

"Excuse me, young man, yes, you, why do you look so upset? Life is not bringing joy and pleasure to you. I'll trade you that miserable soul of yours for constant pleasure and joy. I'll give you what you never had and what you've dreamed of. Think about it. You can have human pleasure. All you have to do is not obey your so-called god."

I turned around to see who was whispering into my ear, telling me those lies. To my surprise, it was a snake. So I replied, "So it's you, the one with the false promises. I remember when I would walk, lost in my human pleasure, being selfish, yet it always made me feel empty."

"Look, you pathetic fool, I will always make you miserable because you're weak and you follow your powerless god, but today, you die."

Running scared, I found a place to hide, then close to me, I heard a voice that was telling me, "Son, bend a knee. Remember I am always here for you. If you pray with faith, anything will be possible because I stand with you."

"Ha ha ha ha I caught up with you, worthless human."

To the snake's surprise, I spread my wings, grab it by the head, and lifted it to the sky, where it was powerless. Slam after slam, suddenly the snake ran away in defeat. My heavenly Father gave me the tools to be victorious through my prayers.

If I stand with my heavenly Father, who can stand against me?

Smile, Someone Needs You

Don't be sad or depressed. The enemy is playing tricks with your mind, making you feel worthless, making you feel like you don't make a difference. God is holding you even though you don't realize it. He has a purpose for you. Look around you. If you have kids, they look up to you. If your parents are old already, they need you. If your friends are on the wrong path, they need you. God has the weapons for you, but you need to get up and show God you really want to make a difference in someone's life. You matter because someone needs you, and to someone, you're worth so much. Keep your head up and remember to make a difference.

God didn't give you another day just to bless you; He gave you another day so you can be a blessing to someone else.

It's All Up to You

It has always been a pleasure to pray and give advice to others, but sometimes we as humans live in a world where we are scared to make a change even if it's for the good of us only because we are comfortable the way we are. Many lived an abusive life but are scared of moving on because we are scared of the future and the outcome. Many always end up living in a circle. They fall in love with the wrong one, leave, and pick another, and let the circle begin spinning over and over because they're scared of being alone. Take your time to know someone first. I can continue going and going with examples, but it's up to you to take the advice. Remember, if you have a long time doing something that is hurting you or you don't like, then I think it's time to get some of that wise advice and do things differently.

And when you can't no more,

Let go and let God. Not even all the advice in the world will help you till you're ready to make changes.

What Do You Feed Yourself?

We tend to feed from others, feed from society, but what are you actually feeding yourself is the question.

I see many people feeding themselves negativity, sadness, and many other things that are harmful and affects them emotionally, spiritually, and, at times, physically.

If you wake up in the morning with the mentality that it's going to be a bad day, you're feeding yourself negativity. Throughout the day, that negativity will become a reality because you believe what you're feeding yourself.

When you're depressed, what are you feeding yourself? Do you start feeding yourself depressing music with depressing quotes. All of that is just like poison to your emotions. It's like giving a knife to a person who likes to cut himself.

You watch TV, and feed from so many fake people that if you saw them without all that makeup, they look sick. You feed yourself the big lie that you need to look a certain way or have so much to be happy and be perfect. In all reality most of them are so busy with their superficial lives that they forget to live. That's exactly what you start to feed yourself when trying to look like something unreal, so what happens? You forget to live.

They say you are what you eat. You eat fats and grease; you can end up in the hospital with clogged arteries. So if you feed off depression; you will be depressed. You feed off negativity; you will be negative. Feed yourself positivity, happiness, and joy. Hard, yes, it is, but not impossible. Read stuff that will help you stay positive. Listen to music that will allow you to be happy and positive.

I am pretty sure you know what happens with your body when you don't drink water. The same happens to your soul when you don't feed from God.

A Real Woman Can Do It All by Herself, But a Real Man Won't Let Her

She is a strong woman, many years without a man, working two jobs. First job from eight to four, now back home to do the hardest job—being a mother. Many foolish men try to make her feel special for a while and get what they want, but they didn't see how smart she is. She has learned to be strong and wise, but she better be careful not to judge every man the same. One day, she might meet that man who will tell her not to worry. He will take charge, let her rest and enjoy life. Not because she can't but because he was raised by a queen, which was his mother, who was mistreated by the world and now knows the struggles of life because of her. Don't make the mistake of making him feel less of a man when he tells you that he will protect and take care of you because all he wants is for you to have a peaceful, restful, and beautiful life.

If you look for happiness in money, you will always be unhappy because you could never have enough.

Make beautiful memories that you treasure together.

Author

Everybody has a story to tell and their own book to write. You are the author, the writer of that book. You decide what stays and what goes. What makes a book interesting are the problems, the drama, the adventures, but at the end, we all expect a beautiful happily ever after, but then you say, "Ha ha ha ha impossible," so I remind you that you stand in front of a father who makes the impossible possible. Learn from your own mistakes so that you won't write the same chapter over and over. Start fresh every day with a clear mind and positive outlook of life that will help you in your life story. Your book could be great with less drama, suffering, and sadness. Then you need to include God in your book, for He will lift you, make your troubles vanish, and make your book a beautiful life story.

Write about love.
Write about faith.
Write about hope.

The Past

Prisoner of your mistakes.
Afraid of ugly memories.
Sadness overcomes your happiness.
Terrible, painful moments.

Many people can't move on in their life because they are prisoners of their past. The past stays behind, no longer available unless you relive it every day in your own mind. I know it's hard to keep on moving on. Learn to forgive so you can be able to breath and be able to move on. Forgive others for the pain they have cause. Forgive yourself. Just remember all of those bad moments and terrible times have made you stronger and wiser, so absorb the good and exhale the bad.

God forgives your sins.

You should forgive your past and move on.

Never be a prisoner of your own thoughts. They are a life lessons, not life sentence.

If Someone Treats You Bad, Remember Something Is Wrong with Them, Not You

Heartbreaks, gossiping, backstabbing, all of these things hurt, I know, I've been through it myself. I've seen so many people, especially women, get hurt. One thing that really gets me sad is to see them hurting for someone not worth those tears. You need to understand. Don't be too hard on yourself just because the other person is the one who is being bad. Who needs to be sad and upset? It's them, for being okay with making other human beings suffer.

Value yourself. God created beautiful princesses, and when you learn to give yourself that place, you better believe your Father, our King, will protect you.

Always smile because many will feed from your sadness. Make people starve when they look at you expecting to find sadness. Let them see your beautiful smile shining with the joy of the Lord. Make them wonder.

Alone

Have you ever felt lonely, unwanted, hopeless, or worthless? These are feelings that are part of being depressed.

You can be around your family, your spouse, or people who love and care for you but still feel alone.

Why? Many things can trigger these feelings; stress, sadness, or even anger. You just want to run and get lost in a place where no one can find you.

You're not alone. Sometimes those emotions get the best of me and many others. I wish I could run to someone and cry like a baby to just let go of my emotions. Only a person who suffers or has suffered from depression understands those feelings and knows how to help someone. That's the reason why I'm here now trying to help others learn how to control those feelings.

1. The best thing to do is relax, meditate, and pray.
2. Give yourself time to cry, for it is not weakness but sadness leaving your body.
3. Try to focus on other things that will distract you from those feelings.
4. Help others who suffer with those same feelings. It will definitely make you feel better.
5. Be kind and help others focus on their needs and try to help them feel better about themselves.

Family Pack

In today's society, I see so many women and men living single with the struggle of finding the right partner. I know it's a struggle not only to find the right partner for you, but if you're a woman or a man who has kids, it's so important to find that person who will love your children like if they were their own. Remember, be patient in finding someone who will love all of you, and when I say all of you, it means you and your kids because those blessings are part of you, so it's a family pack that person needs to either take it all or take none.

There is nothing more heartbreaking than to live with someone who does not love your children. On the other hand, there is nothing more beautiful than to see a woman fixing the hair of a little girl who is not hers, but she treats her like if she is; a woman who will cook for them even when not asked to. What's also beautiful is when a man plays ball or wrestles with little boys who are from a different dad, but to him, he calls them his boys; a man who is willing to teach them right from wrong and guides them.

If you're a person who is dating someone with kids, make sure what you're doing is what you want because at the end, you're not only hurting one person but also the children of that person.

Give yourself time to know someone and how they act around your kids before you even make a big move in your life because it's also the life of your children.

And for those who have partners with children, treat them the way you would like others to treat your children.

Thank you to those who say "my kids" even if they're not biological, but in your eyes, they are.

Gossip

We see it, and we hear it everywhere, at work, at school, at the store, and even at church. Why do we love to feed that toxic habit into ourselves? When a person comes to you and talks bad about someone else, I'll guarantee you, they will be talking about you to someone else too. Gossip destroys families, friendship, marriages, and sometimes business partnerships.

The worst feeling is to hear someone you love talking bad about you to someone else and not because someone told you but because you witnessed it. What can you do? Well, it's simple to say and hard to do but simply just ignore it, for most of these people only want to spread those rumors to make themselves look better or feel better about themselves.

Be wise enough to ignore people talking about you.

Be wise enough to remove yourself from that toxic gossiping circle.

Gossiping only shows the immaturity of a person who is insecure of themselves.

Strong minds discuss ideas.

Average minds discuss events.

Weak minds discuss people.

Who cares what you could've done, should've done, might have done?

What matters is what you're going to do from now on.

She said, "I just think I wasted my life in things that didn't matter."

I looked at her and said, "Well, it is what it is ha ha ha ha ha ha ha!"

She said, "Seriously that's all you got to say?"

I put on my serious face and replied, "Just kidding. Look, it's not how you wasted your life because that's in the past, and just like the river's running water, you won't touch the same water twice because it's gone. What really matters is what you are going to do with your life from now on. Are you planning on focusing on your dreams and goals or do you want to continue wasting your time on things that really don't matter? So if you don't like how life is, keep on moving because you're not a tree."

Hello, Yes, You?

For the heart broken,
For the sick and ill,
For the sad and lonely,
For the anxious and desperate,
For the addicts and lost,
For the atheist and the Christians,
For the forgotten and the sinners,
For everyone who's going through problems or issues,

God loves you, and He's waiting with arms wide open.

O Father, I pray for everyone I mentioned. Help them rest in You. O heavenly Father, I ask that You guide, You protect, You bless and keep all of them healthy. O Lord Jesus Christ, in Your name, I command all illnesses, problems, and issues to banish and burn. O God, help them to stay focused on You alone. Light up their path with the light of Your Holy Spirit so that they be guided in the right direction. O God, let Your Holy Spirit rule in them and kick out everything that is not good for them physically, mentally, and spiritually. O God, bless them today, tomorrow, and forever. O God, thank You because with faith, hope, and love, we will overcome anything that gets in our way. O Lord, bless them and keep them embraced in Your arms, love them, and protect them from evil. In Your name, we pray, Jesus Christ. Amen.

A King

A king is not born wise, but the struggles and problems made him who he is.

Strong, noble, and kind, people love him for the person he is, not because of his power.

But just like any other king, he has downfalls. He has obstacles that he needs to overcome.

His queen knows exactly when he needs her because of her support, he stands firm.

His queen would walk miles if necessary just to see him happy, to see him succeed.

A king loves his queen unconditionally because she always makes him feel secure, motivates him to keep on going. She is sweet, lovely, and caring.

The king walks with confidence because he knows he has a beautiful queen who has his back at time of desperation.

The best king is not the richest, not the smartest, and not the one with popularity, but the one who is kind, noble, wise, and has the best queen and people love him for his actions, not his words.

The best wisdom comes from God.
God bless you always.

Bad Pride

Break free from that bad pride if you're mad at someone and both of you won't say sorry. Be the one who takes the first step to continue on the right path and continue a beautiful relationship. With pride, you suffer in silence. When you are in need of help of any kind, you don't ask the other person because you're too full of yourself. You are so full of pride that you don't let your emotions come out and let people help you, so you've got to swallow your pride.

The three words that you will hardly hear a proud person say are please, sorry, and thank you. These are words that keep our relationships with our families or friends keep on going.

You'd rather give up on people than your own pride. Pride tears friendships and families apart. In addition, people begin to avoid you, talk bad about you because of this negative trait of yours. You have yourself a bad reputation.

Pride will make you lose great opportunities. When you're not humble, no one will want to do business with you or even be part of your life. You lose out on the opportunity to increase your knowledge and skills because pride makes you feel like you know more than anyone who is teaching you.

Pride kills and will destroy a good person's heart. Do you want to continue being avoided by your friends, by your family, losing out on opportunities and facing all the trouble associated with pride? Be humble, and you will see the difference in your relationship with people, friends, and family. Swallow your pride and practice humility today.

Compliments

Who doesn't like compliments?

Complimenting someone will make their day much brighter.

Compliments can be given to you all of your life. If you work, who doesn't like for the boss to tell them, "Thank you for your amazing work? Makes you want to go back the next day, and try even harder because of that small compliment that created motivation. But sadly, most of the time, we hear more of the tiny little mistake we made, and they take for granted all the hard work we do. Compliments in your love relationship is a must to keep that attraction alive. An "oh wow, you look so beautiful, baby," can spark that flame back up. When a man only criticizes and puts down his significant other, he better believe someone else's compliments will, little by little, pull her apart from him. To a woman, a million compliments by different men can be said, but to her, the only compliment that matters never was said (his).

The best compliments are the ones that you give yourself because it shows you finally learn to love yourself first.

Don't let a man's compliments get to your head, for most are said to get something out of you. Don't let judgment get to your heart, for no one has the right to judge.

My compliment to all of you ladies is that you're beautiful because my Father and God created you beautiful and unique.

Time

If I asked you to sell me one year of your life, would you? Don't waste your life.

Time, just like death, don't discriminate. They pass by without looking at who gets hurt, who gets old, or who dies.

How much time do you have? Well, you have infinite time but not infinite life till the Lord comes or till it's time to say your last goodbye, then you can have eternal life.

Just like a river's flow, you can't ever touch the same water. You won't see the same day.

What takes the most time out of your life? Make sure you are wasting your time on things that are worth wasting it on, your life, your kids, your family, your friends, or whatever matters to you the most, but most importantly, give your time to God because He gives you time and life. Just remember you're not only wasting time, you're wasting life. If you're reading this, let my Lord multiply your time because you're giving me a piece of it by using some of your minutes to read this, I really appreciate it.

She Don't Believe in Love

Her smile was beautiful, when I looked into her eyes, the goodness of my heart could penetrate through her eyes.

I could see her pain. I could see her hurting. I could see more than just her smile.

I asked, "So how's life?" She replied, "Just fine." She also asked how mine was.

I asked her why her eyes were full of sadness and pain.

"I could see pass that beautiful smile. I know you don't believe in love any more.

Many men have played with your heart, hurt your feelings, and did you wrong.

Let me hold you tight. Let me show you a new beginning.

Let me be the hope you were waiting for. Don't stop believing in love because men were cruel.

Let me be the one who introduces you to a beautiful unconditional, true love."

A man who loves God will offer you great love, for he understands what a woman is worth in the eyes of God.

Kiss

A gentleman will kiss your hand, for he admirers you and respects you.

A friends will kiss your cheeks.

A family member will embrace you and kiss your cheeks out of love and care.

Like a father kisses his babies on the head with all his tender love.

Your significant other will kiss your forehead, not only because of love but meaning they will return.

Kisses all over your face means that he loves every small part of your beautiful face.

Kisses on your mouth means I love you.

But few can really experience the soulmate kiss. Your eyes interlock with each other, and you get lost in each other while your souls are passionately kissing without a single touch of your body.

Show people your feelings with a hug and a kiss.

Wrong Love

The world we live in now is blinded by lies manipulated by society. This world is used to seeing love, and they forgot about true love, the love that you can feel.

"Look, babe, I bought you a new car. See, I love you."

"Look, a new diamond ring for you to show you my love."

What happens after the surprise and the enchantment is gone? Where is the love now? In another new thing?

Let me tell you about real love, the one you can't see but you can feel.

The love that you feel when your loved one surprises you at work, just to caress your face.

The love you feel when your loved one asks if you got to your destination safe.

The love you feel when your loved one asks if you ate or if you slept good or how's your day going?

The love you feel by an embrace or a long hug, maybe a kiss on the forehead. But there is no bigger feeling of love than to know your loved one is praying for you.

I'd rather feel love than to see love.

Moon

Sitting outside with tears in my eyes, contemplating the beauty of your brightness, I know she will be contemplating you too.

Only if you could talk and let her know how you feel inside. I wish I was just like a howling wolf. I want to release my emotions and my pain that runs deep inside because you are not around.

I know you feel lonely when the sun is not around. Oh please, use your beautiful glow to light up her night because I know she is suffering too. Sometimes loneliness strike, and we miss our better half. The best thing we can do is ask God to give us the strength and give them the strength to relieve their pain.

Money

Money can buy you a huge house, but only love turns it into a home.

Money can buy you an expensive watch but won't buy you time to enjoy the lovely moments.

Money can buy you thousands of books but can't buy you wisdom to write a lovely story.

Money can buy you medicine but can't buy you life.

Money can buy you sex but won't buy you love.

Treasure everything that comes to you with love.

When you die, no one will stand in front of your grave and say, "He had a great watch and a beautiful car." When you die, people will miss you for the love you showed them.

Love equals God, God is greater than money.

Heart Broken

She trusted you, gave you all her love and dedication. All you ever did was repay her with suffering and tortured her heart.

You left and left her heart broken. Now she doesn't want to trust or love.

So I am sitting here trying to put the broken pieces of her heart together. She is broken but not incomplete. To me, she is worth every minute that was taken away from my life.

What kind of man cuts the wings of a beautiful butterfly just to watch it die?

I'll be patient because she deserves the most beautiful things in life. She may be heart-broken, but she doesn't stand alone. You dethroned this beautiful queen, but I'll give her a better kingdom.

God bless you, ladies, put your trust in God, not in men, for men will let you down and disappoint you often. Let God bring you the man you deserve. Patience.

Insecurity

Don't let your insecurities drown you, rip you, and pull you apart. Don't let society feed your insecurities and poison your brain with man-made people. Don't let people's insults control your emotions and trigger your insecurities. Stop wondering if you will ever be happy with yourself. Stop wondering that if you're not happy with yourself, then nobody will be happy with you. Don't let insecurities get you paranoid. Remember there is always someone asking God for someone just like you. God created you amazingly just the way you are. Breathe confidence and exhale all your insecurities. Next time you look at yourself in the mirror, remember you're looking at God's creation, beautiful and wonderful.

Circumstances

Circumstances affect us. Sometimes circumstances are out of our control. How you live today is part of the circumstances that took place in the past. Many circumstances can be life changing for example, getting married, a divorce, losing a loved one, a new job, even a new house. Some circumstances are bad, but you shouldn't let those circumstances affect the positive side of your life. We can't control some of the upcoming circumstances we will experience, but we can definitely control how we react to them. Remember when circumstances are good, enjoy them. When the circumstances are bad, learn from them.

Sending you tons of blessings.

Her Smile

He said, "Bro, look at her beautiful smile."

What you see is not what it looks like. Look deep into her eyes and go deep into her soul, only there you will see.

Her beautiful smile is not because of joy but to mask the pain in her heart.

Her beautiful smile is not because of happiness but to mask the sadness she drags.

Every day, when she walks out of her home, she puts on her happy mask to hide her sorrows.

Her smile fools you to believe her life is perfect, but she has been through verbal abuse, mental abuse, and physical abuse.

You don't see how hard she tries not to break down 'cause all her broken pieces would fall.

She walks head up and confident, but her sadness is torturing her.

Her smile can light up a room, but her heart is full of darkness.

She stops trusting because every man lets her down.

She looks strong and beautiful. She can intimidate men with her smile, but inside her, she just wants to feel loved, wants to feel safe, and she wants to feel protected.

Learn to look at her soul, and you will have the key to her heart.

Her smile is to shield and guard herself from guys like you, bro.

Ladies, know that you're not alone. Yes, the road is hard, but a man died for you because he loves you more than you imagine. Put your focus on God; He will put your broken heart and your broken pieces together. He will heal you and keep you protected. Be blessed always.

Perseverance

By perseverance, the snail reached the ark. The snail, not only has perseverance, it also has patience. The snail did not say, "Wow, it's far." The snail looked up and said, "O Lord, here I come." Perseverance. It's an element that develops your character. Perseverance, it's your resolution, constancy, and your endurance. If you can't run, then walk. If you can't walk, then crawl. What matters is that you don't stop, and if you stop, make sure it's to help someone get up. Just like a river cuts through rock not because of its strength but because of its constancy. Many things come hand in hand. If you don't believe in yourself, you can't have perseverance. If you fail, don't discourage yourself. Learn and try again. My major example of perseverance has been becoming Christian. It's been the biggest challenge a man from the world can accomplish, but with faith, hope, and perseverance, we can get there. Regardless of your failures, regardless of the pain or how many times you fall, God doesn't want us to get there fast but to just get there. Look always forward. Keep on the move. Remember the only one who can stop you is you.

Have perseverance.

Have faith.

Don't give up.

Mesmerize

Gazing into the night sky, full of twinkling pretty stars, and now I can't stop thinking about your beautiful eyes.

Mesmerized by the beauty of your precious face that infinitely captivates my mind.

At a loss of words to explain how beautiful you are, I know there is not one thing I would change.

The enchantment of your gorgeous smile lights up my world when it's dark and lonely.

Your precious hands hold the key to my humble heart that skips a beat when I hear your name.

When God Sends You the Man You Were Called To Be With

This is so deep, beautiful, and true. Be patient. The feeling will be amazing because for once, it won't be your choice but God's choice. Then and only then you will see the difference in how you are loved and appreciated. Any man will want your flesh, but a man whom God has for you will look deep into your eyes and want to feel your soul connect to his. Be patient, have faith, and believe he's real, just wait and see. When you finally get him, hold him, embrace him, and don't let him go because if God sends him, it was to bless you, protect you, and love you unconditionally.

Be patient.

Your Soul

I am looking at your soul, not only your body, even though you're gorgeous, even though you're precious, and even though you're beautiful. I am looking at your soul because your body will wrinkle, your body and face will age, but your soul won't. I am looking at your soul for when the time comes, we will hold hands and together live forever in eternity, sitting in the clouds, where God will embrace us forever. If a man loves a woman's soul, he will end up loving one woman.

She Said

Why are you always telling me to eat?
Why are you always telling me to buckle up when I leave?
Why do you always get mad when I text and drive?
Why do you always pray so much for me?
Why do you want to call me so much when I am away?

He replied,
Because I care, and I love you so much. When I don't do those things anymore, worry because it means I am gone. But for now, let me care and let me love you.

Treat Her Like One

If a man expects his woman to be like an angel in his life, then he should first create heaven for her. But in order for a man to create a heavenlike environment for his precious angel, he first needs to know and understand God. He needs to ask for His guidance of what he should do to make a little heaven on earth for his precious angel. Once the man has God's guidance, he should be able to guide her and push her to God. Once he has God's wisdom, he will be able to treat her like one.

Hearts

There is a Spanish saying, "Faces, we see. Heart, we don't know."
There are hearts in trouble,
Hearts that envy,
Hearts with rage,
Hearts that suffer,
Hearts that hate,
Hearts that betray,
Hearts in pain,
Hearts that are scarred.
There are good hearts,
Hearts with joy,
Hearts that forgive,
Hearts that cherish,
Hearts that lift,
Hearts that help.
But there is a heart that is pure and full of unconditional love, that's the heart of Jesus Christ! When you find it, you will be blessed forever!

You're Eyes

Trying to find my way back to reality, lost in the beauty of your deep gorgeous eyes. It's not the sparkle nor the shine, it's the peace I feel when I get lost in them. I feel tranquility and serenity that calms my insanity. I thank you not only for letting me feel at peace but for letting me touch your soul when my eyes get lost in yours, the moment that you open the door of your eyes to me.

Life

*L*ove every day like it's your last.
*I*nspire and motivate others around you.
*F*orgive those who have hurt you.
*E*ncourage others to keep on going.

Ladies, if a Man Is Not Following God, He's Not Right to Lead You

When a man follows God, he learns so many beautiful things but the major thing is love. Love consists of care, protection, and respect. A man who follows God learns that in order to be a great leader, he needs to be a good servant for others and for his significant other. A man who follows God learns discipline, learns to obey the rules. A man who follows God will guide her to God. A man of God will protect her, make her feel safe, make her feel loved. The man will let God take control of their life because he knows God will guide them to a better living and a peaceful life.

I Am with You

I want to dedicate this poem to all mothers who have lost a child, a baby, a son, a daughter, and to all unborn babies. To all mothers, let my Lord bless you always.

Here it goes.

My mom lost a baby that if today he were to be alive, he would've been older than me.

I am with you.

I know at times you close your eyes and think about life and me.

Don't worry, for I am with you always.

That soft breeze that caresses your face, it's me running my fingers through your cheeks.

When you say you can't see me, look up at the sky and know that I am looking straight at you from heaven above.

Don't be too hard on yourself. I am enjoying myself in this beautiful paradise next to God.

I want you to be strong, I know it's hard. I miss you too, but you need to be a motivation for all those who also look up to you.

Don't be scared. I'll lighten up the path, just look at the stars, and I will show you the way.

I know you spend sleepless nights thinking why. Well, don't see it that way, for this place is better than the world.

When you feel depressed and alone, close your eyes and relax. Remember I am with you in good and bad.

Remember people see it as you lost a child, but in reality, you gained an angel.

I love and forever I am with you.

What Is Your Addiction? What Medicine Takes Your Pain Away?

My mother used to drink for three days straight. I would see her crying. I would ask, "Why do you drink, Mom?" She would say, "To forget."

I know many people who say they drink to forget, but in reality, they don't need to temporarily forget. They need to forgive and let go of the past that only weighs them down. Need to free themselves from everything that's causing pain and suffering in order to feel at peace.

Why do we get addicted to things that not only hurt us but hurt everyone around us, the people who love us? People tend to fall into drinking or drug addiction 'cause they lost a brother, a sister, the mother, the father, a loved one. But ask yourselves a question? Do you really think that loved one would've liked to see you drunk, drugged, angry, or depressed? Your family suffers because they care, they love you, they want what's best for you. I suffered a lot seeing my dad and mom drunk. I suffered so much when I lost my dad at age eighteen. I wasted three years in depression because I was young and unguided. We can drink all the alcohol in the world, use all drugs, or cut our skin all we want, but if it's not in us to let go of what is holding us down to move on, we will continue the same. I've seen and heard so many testimonies, and I am proof that the only solution to a better living is God. Trust and walk by faith, and God will guide you and take that pain away. All you have to do is let go and let God.

Hollow Space

We all have a hollow space in us, a space that some fill up with drugs, alcohol, sex, food, and anything that tends to keep us satisfied and happy momentarily. Once you feel full and satisfied, your problems, stress, worries, pain, sadness, and negativity tend to return to eat and feed from those things again. Wake up, please realize that those things are leaving you feeling empty again and becoming a cycle. Well, I was once in that cycle, then I filled up my hollow space with God and His amazing love. It was like a cure. I haven't seen that hollow space. My worries are gone. I feel positive all the time and happy 'cause now I have Christ in my heart. You decide what you fill up your hollow space with, just make sure you don't end up empty again.

A Million Ways to Say I Love You

The little things always count. It's beautiful to know someone loves and cares enough to know if you already ate, if you had a good day at work, make sure that you're not texting and driving, and if you slept good. There are many ways to show your love and affection for others. Always do little things that shows them you are always loving them and thinking of them. Do the things money can't buy.

You Are God's Masterpiece

Know who you are. Value, love, and care for yourself. If someone talks bad about you, don't let it get to you. Don't take it so serious because you are not only God's masterpiece, you're a child of God. Whatever the world has to say shouldn't matter, for this world is moved by the evil one, and he only wants to see us down. Sometimes our biggest mistake is to give that power to them by letting their gossip get to us. At times when it really gets to us it might be because it may be true so we need to change our behaviors or attitudes.

Change

Sometimes you try and try, but life does not go as you plan. The solution would be to change the way you will see life. By that, I mean turn to Christ, and you would see the wonderful change. At one point, my life was not going the way I wanted it to go, so I turned to Christ. So now my life is worry-free, stress-free, and positive all the time because of the way I see life now. All thanks and glory to my Lord and Savior God.

My Rose

A world full of flowers in different gardens standing out amongst the
flowers.

The single most beautiful rose, breathtaking to see her beauty, it is
mesmerizing.

The brilliant glow only God can give, her petals are soft to the touch.

I don't see no imperfections. I can only see the beauty that radiates.

I don't want to look anywhere else. The perfect rose, I have found.

It caught my attention not only her external beauty but her internal soul.

Now that I hold her, I carry her with love respect and care.

She is precious and incomparable to any other.

I will hold her next to my heart because now she is my rose.

The Hurtful Word

There are three things that you can't recover in life. The hurtful word after it's said, the moment after it's missed, and the time after it's gone.

1. Be careful what you say especially when angry, mad, or even stressed out.
2. Treasure even the smallest moments 'cause they make amazing memories.
3. Don't rush life, take it slow, relax, breathe, enjoy every second of it.

Every second that we live is just like the rivers running water you will never ever touch it again.

The Penguin

When a male penguin finds a female penguin, he looks in the entire beach for the perfect pebble to present to her. Amazing as it is, these precious little animals show us that it's not the size of the gift nor how much it's worth but the significance of it. To us, it's just a simple rock or pebble. To them, it's finding the perfect rock to show all his love, stating that he finds in her the soulmate he's been looking for. Whatever you decide to give your wife or girlfriend, do it with a meaning that will stay in both of your hearts.

The Younger You

I can see how much you love this woman.

I can see how much you admire this woman.

I can see how much you would like to be her again because you see her younger and perfect.

I don't dislike her.

But she is not perfect.

She wouldn't probably get my attention.

But I do thank her because of her,

I found you.

I found my perfect woman.

And even though you feel imperfect, your heart has changed, your persona has changed, and even the ability to see life in a different way has changed.

And even though many would say, "Do you regret not finding her sooner?"

And as I hold you in my arms, tears fall because I realize that this time was chosen by God, so it was the perfect time.

I don't want you younger.

I don't want you thinner.

I don't want you richer.

You are perfect.

And you know why.

Because I agape love you, I love you with the unconditional love that comes from the heart of God.

He Didn't Know What He Had

My friend and I were talking, and he was saying he didn't understand his wife. So he asked me a question, "Can you describe the perfect woman?" So I said, "Well, a perfect woman for me would be a woman who is not only beautiful inside and out but also sweet and understanding, will cheer you up when you're down. She will stand next to you in good and bad. She will give you her 100 percent. She will push you so you can succeed. She will communicate with you to have a better relationship. She will laugh at your jokes even when they are not funny. She will cook your favorite dish just so she can see you smile. She will support you all the way." He was amused by my answer, so he replied, "Wow, I need a woman like that." So I told him, "Run home and appreciate your wife because that's whom I just describe."

The Love in Us

Hard to explain
How can two strangers
With different life views
Come together
Not only to love each other
But to be deeply in love with each other

People call it crazy
Because they can't understand
That two strangers
Have come together
To teach the world
That it's not only to love
But the main adjective are the words *in love*
Rooted to the heart not only their heart but
The foundation of *love* which is God because God is perfect *love*.

Wear Love Everywhere You Go

Wear love everywhere you go 'cause love overpowers hate. Give love to the whole world. Love your friends, love your family, love even your enemy. I know a lot of people who like to fight back, but they only make the problem bigger.

1. When you fight back, you're giving that other person satisfaction.
2. When you fight back, you only make things worse.
3. Why do you fight back? 'Cause you're angry, sad, upset? See those are not good feelings to react from.

Always send your blessings to all of those who curse you, and you will see the difference in you and them. Hate will never give you good results in life. Love yourself, love the people around you, and most importantly, love God (Colossians 3:14).

Letter to Him

Hello.

I know it may sound crazy, but I am writing you this letter to say thank you.

Thank you for setting her free.

Thank you for not taking care of her.

Thank you for not giving her the attention she deserves.

Thank you for taking her for granted.

Thank you for not appreciating her.

Thank you for ignoring her.

When she was at your side, you were a lucky man, but now that she is by my side, I am a blessed man.

When I say thank you, it's because

When you set her free, I was able to show her the beauty of being in love again.

She is in good hands now.

Not only my hands but God's hands too.

Arise and Shine!

I pray and declare that every woman around the world reading this book be set free from every lie that the enemy might have put in your head, heart, and soul. I declare that the Holy Spirit comes over you and fills you with His truth and glory. May you not lean unto your own understanding but in all things trust in the Lord with all of your heart. Believe what His word says about you. Arise, beautiful daughter of Zion, in all of God's glory. Dress yourself in righteousness, peace, and joy in the Holy Spirit. Again, I say arise and shine, for the glory of the Lord has risen upon you. *It's time to arise. Amen. God be with you always.*

Acknowledgments

First and most important, I want to give all the glory to God. Without Him, this book wouldn't be in existence. I want to thank Veronica Galvez for her time, guidance, and motivation. My uncle, Jose Hernandez, for his faith in me. Everyone who has supported and prayed for me. Thanks to pastors Ivan Elizarraraz and Mauro Davalos. Thanks to everyone who was waiting for this book to become a reality and everyone who enjoys my post on Facebook. One flesh, one heart, one love, one God.

About the Author

Eduardo Vallecillo was born in El Paso, Texas. He lived in Juarez, Mexico, up until he was about eleven years old. He is a father of six wonderful children. His passion is to transform and impact lives through his life experiences and revelation that has been given to him from the heart of God for people of all walks of life. His desire is to encourage and help people understand their identity as they get closer to God through his writings.

Eduardo Vallecillo is an evangelist at heart and is a servant of the Lord Most High. He looks for any opportunity to serve and to preach the gospel in the streets to see souls saved and delivered. His vision is to save souls, help the poor, and open up food pantries and orphanages all over the world.

The cry of his heart is "Lord, let Your kingdom come, let Your will be done on earth as it is in heaven." The Lord has given him much knowledge, wisdom, and understanding in many areas of life. It is evident that the Lord has called and ordained him ever since he was in his mother's womb for such a time as this.

CPSIA information can be obtained
at www.ICGtesting.com
Printed in the USA
BVHW070241160222
629080BV00003B/510